Saint John Vianney

Saint John Vianney

A Priest for All People

Written by Elizabeth Marie DeDomenico, FSP
Illustrated by Ben Hatke

Pauline
BOOKS & MEDIA
Boston

Library of Congress Cataloging-in-Publication Data

DeDomenico, Elizabeth Marie.
  Saint John Vianney : a priest for all people / written by
Elizabeth Marie DeDomenico ; illustrated by Ben Hatke.
    p. cm. — (Encounter the saints series)
  ISBN 0-8198-7115-X (pbk.)
  1.   Vianney, Jean Baptiste Marie, Saint, 1786–1859—
Juvenile literature. 2. Christian saints—France—Ars (Ain)—
Biography—Juvenile literature. 3.   Catholic Church—
France—Ars (Ain)—Clergy—Biography—Juvenile literature.
I. Hatke, Ben. II. Title.
  BX4700.V5D43 2008
  282.092—dc22
  [B]
                                        2008020946

"P" and PAULINE are registered trademarks of the Daughters
of St. Paul.

Published by Pauline Books & Media, 50 Saint Pauls
Avenue, Boston, MA 02130-3491

Printed in the U.S.A.

www.pauline.org

Pauline Books & Media is the publishing house of the
Daughters of St. Paul, an international congregation of
women religious serving the Church with the communica-
tions media.

1 2 3 4 5 6 7 8 9   13 12 11 10 09 08

Encounter the Saints Series

Blesseds Jacinta and Francisco Marto
Shepherds of Fatima

Blessed Pier Giorgio Frassati
Journey to the Summit

Blessed Teresa of Calcutta
Missionary of Charity

Journeys with Mary
Apparitions of Our Lady

Saint Anthony of Padua
Fire and Light

Saint Bakhita of Sudan
Forever Free

Saint Bernadette Soubirous
Light in the Grotto

Saint Edith Stein
Blessed by the Cross

Saint Elizabeth Ann Seton
Daughter of America

Saint Faustina Kowalska
Messenger of Mercy

Saint Frances Xavier Cabrini
Cecchina's Dream

Saint Francis of Assisi
Gentle Revolutionary

Saint Ignatius of Loyola
For the Greater Glory of God

Saint Isaac Jogues
With Burning Heart

Saint Joan of Arc
God's Soldier

Saint John Vianney
A Priest for All People

Saint Juan Diego
And Our Lady of Guadalupe

Saint Katharine Drexel
The Total Gift

Saint Martin de Porres
Humble Healer

Saint Maximilian Kolbe
Mary's Knight

Saint Paul
The Thirteenth Apostle

Saint Pio of Pietrelcina
Rich in Love

Saint Teresa of Ávila
Joyful in the Lord

Saint Thérèse of Lisieux
The Way of Love

For other children's titles on the saints,
visit our Web site: www.pauline.org

CONTENTS

1

LIFE BEFORE THE REVOLUTION

"I want it!" Marguerite demanded fierce-
ly, stamping her feet to get her brother's
attention. "I don't have one."

"No, it's my rosary. You can't have it,"
John answered back.

"Give it to me, John," Marguerite insisted.
She tried to grab the rosary beads away from
her older brother. John was four years old and
Marguerite just eighteen months younger.

John held tightly onto the rosary, but
Marguerite's screams grew louder. John did
not know what to do, so he did what most
children his age would do: he ran to his
mother.

"Mama!" he pleaded. "Tell her that it
belongs to me."

Madame Vianney was busy preparing
the family meal. She tried to hide her
amusement as she looked down at his
outraged face.

"John, please let your sister hold the
rosary."

John fought back his tears and turned to
his sister.

"Here you are, Gothon," he said, calling her by the family nickname. "You can hold it. But you're really supposed to pray with it. It's not a toy."

Marguerite was beaming now and ran off with the rosary. Madame Vianney smiled at her son.

"John, it was very nice of you to share the rosary with Gothon."

She went over to the chimney and took down a wooden statue of the Blessed Mother.

"Here, this statue is for you, darling."

John's tears dried quickly as he took the little statue into his hands. He had often looked up at it, but he had never dared to take it down or touch it. Now it was his very own! From then on, the statue of Mary became his constant companion. He took her to the fields, around the house, and kept her beside his bed at night.

Not long after, John took his statue one evening and went outside. No one noticed that he was gone. When Madame Vianney realized he wasn't in the house, she began to look all over for him.

"Have you seen John?" she asked his eleven-year-old sister Catherine. "It's growing dark outside, and I can't find him anywhere."

"No, Mother," answered Catherine. "Although the last time I saw him, he was toting his little statue around with him."

"Well, I'm going outside to look for him. If your father comes in, tell him where I am."

Madame Vianney started looking in the yard, and then she remembered the stable. What if John had fallen down and hurt himself? She became more and more worried as she thought of all the possible things that could have happened to her little boy. She stopped short when she caught sight of him in the corner of the stable. He was on his knees praying devoutly before his little Madonna.

"Dear Mary, you are my mother in heaven. I love you very much...."

"John! Here you are," Madame Vianney cried as she embraced him. "Why are you hiding like this? We'll pray together after supper."

"I'm sorry, Mama," John answered. He hadn't meant to scare her. "I didn't know you were looking for me. I won't do it again."

"It's all right, John," said his mother gently. *I can't believe he was out here praying!* she thought. *I usually have to plead with the children to say their prayers. There is something special about this little one. I wonder what he will be like when he grows up...*

❖ ❖ ❖

In 1790, country life in Dardilly, France, should have been peaceful and serene. Matthieu and Marie Vianney were farmers, like their parents and grandparents before them. God had blessed them with a beautiful family of six children. Besides his sisters Catherine and Marguerite, John also had two brothers, François and Cadet. Another sibling, Jeanne-Marie, had died as a young child. The Vianney farm and home were located in the woods and hills not far from the city of Lyon. Together the family worked in the fields and took care of the animals. When the children's chores were finished each day, they loved to play games and have fun. They attended Mass each Sunday with their parents and received instruction in the Catholic faith.

But the world they knew was quickly changing around them. The French Revolution was just beginning. In the years ahead, the rebellion would lead to the violent Reign of Terror, a revolt against the king and the upper classes of society.

Young John, of course, knew nothing of what was happening in the world. He was content to learn his prayers and attend church at his mother's side. The boy was fascinated with everything there—the tabernacle and crucifix, the sound of the church bells, the ceremonies. Above all, the sight of his mother praying so earnestly before the Blessed Sacrament impressed him.

But the parishioners of Dardilly were soon to feel the chilling effects of the bloody revolution sweeping throughout France.

2

A Secret First Communion

Father Jacques Rey, the pastor (or Curé as he was called in French) of the Vianney family's little country church, had recently left the parish after many years. The new bishop of Lyons had sent a replacement, but somehow this new pastor seemed different.

John didn't understand what was happening at the church, but his twelve-year-old sister Catherine was worried about something. He could hear her whispering to his mother.

"This new Curé is always talking about the constitution and our duties as citizens," Catherine complained to her mother. "He often criticizes the priests who served here before he arrived. Have you noticed that the people who come to church are different, too? Some parishioners no longer come, and there are new people we've never seen before."

"Yes, we are living in difficult times," Madame Vianney responded. "With this terrible revolution and French blood flowing so freely, I'm not surprised that we are feeling the effects even in God's own house. Who knows where this all could lead?"

Their fears were confirmed when a relative came to visit. When she heard about the new Curé at Dardilly she spoke up at once. "But doesn't everyone know, Marie? This new priest has taken an oath of allegiance to the revolutionary government. That means he is no longer faithful to the Catholic Church. You must not attend Mass at your church anymore."

Madame Vianney was horrified. Could this be true? There was only one way to find out: she decided to call on the new priest.

"Good afternoon, Monsieur le Curé," Madame Vianney smiled as she stood on the pastor's doorstep.

"Why, Madame Vianney. What a pleasure! Please come in." The Curé led her into the parlor and offered her a glass of water. Madame Vianney accepted and politely complimented the pastor on his most recent sermon. She was trying to build up the courage to ask him about the oath of allegiance. She had to know for sure. But she had to be careful. Publicly opposing the oath could be dangerous....

"I'm so glad you appreciated the sermon. It was rather good, wasn't it?" the

Curé chuckled, pouring himself some water as well.

This is going well, thought Madame Vianney. *Now's my chance.*

"It's so reassuring to have strong leadership in our church during these confusing times," Madame Vianney said. "One hears so many strange things; it's difficult to know what is right and what is wrong anymore. For instance, I only recently heard about some kind of oath that the new government is asking our priests to take. Do you know anything about it? I'm sure I can't make heads or tails out of such a thing!"

"Oh, I wouldn't worry about things like that if I were you, Madame Vianney," the Curé said. "The oath of allegiance is harmless. It's just something we have to do nowadays. It would be foolish not to— opposing the oath makes one look like an enemy of the Revolution. Far better to be here at the parish in Dardilly than imprisoned in the Bastille! But don't worry. It's really not important."

"Oh, I'm sure you're right," she smiled, trying not to choke on her water. "It's probably of no importance whatsoever."

As she walked home a short time later, Madame Vianney could not believe what she had just heard. How could he not think this was important? Taking any kind of oath was dreadfully important! And the Curé's first responsibility was to God, not to the Revolution! *What are we to do now?* she thought. *Where can we attend Mass if not at our own parish church?* Tears came to her eyes as she thought of the church where she had been married and her children had been baptized. Filled with sadness, she returned home. Now she would have to explain the situation to her family.

"There is a terrible persecution against the priests who have resisted this oath," Madame Vianney explained, gathering her children around her. "They have to remain in hiding and say Mass secretly to avoid arrest. There are some of these faithful priests traveling from place to place. We must now attend Mass in secret, too."

John was only five years old, but he nodded his head. When the family set out together one evening to attend a secret Mass, John went along eagerly. He trudged across the fields with everyone else and didn't even seem to get tired. Catherine and François, his older sister and brother, were surprised at his energy. Little Marguerite was very sleepy and kept lagging behind.

*John's First Communion, celebrated in secret,
changed his life forever.*

Monsieur Vianney ended up carrying her most of the way!

At long last, they entered what seemed to be a barn. It was so dark they could hardly see where they were going. A kind but weary-looking stranger came to welcome them. Other people were arriving also. Some went off to a corner of the barn, where they waited patiently to confess their sins.

After that, preparations for Mass began. The glow of the candles cast a light on the priest's face as he set out the missal and chalice. Then he put on his wrinkled vestments. It didn't look like much, but the chance to celebrate the Eucharist together meant everything to the people gathered in the dimly-lit barn. Their faith gave them hope and courage as their nation endured the storms of revolution and war.

Eventually the authorities closed the Vianneys' regular parish church, and the family continued to attend Mass in secret. Faithful priests traveled throughout the area to celebrate the Liturgy. To avoid suspicion, they sometimes took on other jobs—Father Groboz worked as a cook, and Father Balley carried carpenter tools. The people of Dardilly worried about the priests' safety. When would this end?

One day in 1797, Father Groboz stopped by the Vianney farm to hear confessions. Afterward, he stayed for supper with the family.

"Believe me, I really *can* cook, Madame Vianney!" Father Groboz insisted. "I've been getting a lot of practice, you know. My *cassoulet* is out of this world!"

Madame Vianney was not impressed.

"That's all very well when you're under-cover, Father. But in *my* house, *I* do the cook-ing. Heaven knows you do enough for us!" She smiled as she ushered him from the kitchen and put the final touches on their supper.

As the family talked that evening, Father Groboz was impressed by young John, who eagerly listened to the priest's every word.

"How old are you now?" Father Groboz asked, turning toward John.

"I'm already eleven years old, Father," he announced proudly.

"How long has it been since you went to confession?"

"Too long!" interjected one of John's older brothers.

"François!" exclaimed Madame Vianney.

"I haven't made my first confession yet," John admitted.

"Well, then," Father Groboz said firmly, "let's take care of that at once."

He took John aside, and the boy made his first confession right then and there. As Father Groboz listened to John confess his sins, he could tell that John wanted to grow in his relationship with God. So Father Groboz suggested that John receive more instruction in the faith, in preparation for his first Communion. His parents agreed, and the following year, John went to live with his aunt in Ecully, which was just two and a half miles south of Dardilly. A group of children there were secretly being prepared to receive their first Communion. John was only there for a few months but he was thrilled to have such an opportunity. He wanted to prepare well for his first Communion—and it became a day that he would remember throughout his life.

It was early in the morning during harvest time in June 1799. John dressed himself quickly and joined his family who had come from Dardilly to celebrate with him. They started out as the first light of dawn was spreading across the sky. John was excited and happy. This was the long-awaited day!

The Vianney family arrived at a large house, surrounded by empty fields, in Ecully. Fathers Groboz had chosen this very spot because of its remote location. Other groups of people were arriving as well, but to the outsider everything appeared very ordinary. John and the other children gathered together in one of the larger rooms. The boys received armbands. John saw that the mothers pulled out Communion veils from under their cloaks for the girls. Each child also received a lighted candle to carry.

Father Groboz had planned every detail of the ceremony. He had even arranged to have carts full of hay placed against the windows of the house to hide all the activity from prying eyes.

Finally, after so much waiting, John went up to receive Jesus in Communion. His heart was bursting with happiness.

First Communion would bring about a lasting effect not only on John's relationship with God, but on the rest of his life as well.

3

FOLLOWING GOD'S CALL

John stopped to wipe the sweat off his forehead. His older brother François was ahead of him, plowing the ground with such speed. He made it look easy! The strong, burly oxen pulling John's plow snorted. John thought they seemed eager to catch up with François' team. He sighed. There was so much work to do: harvesting and haymaking, gathering grapes, taking care of the cattle, pruning trees, digging trenches—and plowing the fields, of course. He was thirteen years old and had just returned home after receiving his first Communion. It was hard to get back into the routine of farm life after months of study.

When the sun finally sank and John was able to return home, he collapsed onto a chair.

"Oh, what a day," he groaned in frustration. "I just can't keep up with François."

Madame Vianney turned to her elder son: "François, can't you give your brother a hand? He isn't that strong yet, you know."

François put down the cup he was drinking from. "Of course he can't work as quickly as I do yet, Mama, but it wouldn't make sense for both of us to work so slowly!"

When John went back to the fields the next day, he brought his little statue of Mary with him. He kissed it and then threw it ahead of him. Then he urged his team of oxen on and plowed until he reached the statue. Picking it up, he threw the statue again. When John returned home that evening, his mother noticed that he didn't seem as discouraged as he had the day before.

"How did your day go?" she asked him.

"Much better," John answered at once. "Mary helped me to keep up with François today!"

❖ ❖ ❖

While ordinary days were unfolding in the village of Dardilly, extraordinary events were happening in other parts of France. The Catholic Church and the French government signed an agreement, and on April 18, 1801, the bells of the great church of Notre Dame rang out loud and clear over Paris after ten years of silence. A new emperor, Napoleon Bonaparte, came into power. Under his rule, religious peace was finally restored to the country.

Father Rey returned to his old parish in Dardilly. The church doors opened wide to welcome all the faithful parishioners who had been worshiping in secret. Now they could participate freely in all the sacred ceremonies just as they had done before.

Fifteen-year-old John longed to be in church, and at every opportunity he would find his way there. Even when the long hours of work in the fields kept him away, he found time to pray. Late at night, he would read from the Gospels or the *Imitation of Christ*. The desire to become a priest began to grow steadily within him. How could his dream ever come true?

One day, John had the courage to talk to his mother about his hopes for the future. "Mama," he said earnestly, "if I become a priest, I could bring many people to God. I know it would be a great sacrifice for the family, but...."

"I had a feeling you would ask me this one day," his mother smiled.

John thought he saw tears in her eyes.

"I think that God is calling you too," she said. "There is nothing I would want more for you. But you must speak to your father."

It wasn't easy to approach his father, because John knew that Matthieu Vianney would not approve of his son's decision. When the youth finally did bring up the subject, his father refused at once.

"How could you even think of such a thing?" Monsieur Vianney answered sternly. "You know I need you here to help on the farm. Who would pay for all your education? It is impossible."

John bowed his head so that his father wouldn't see the tears streaming down his face. He went away sad, but he kept silent. For the next two years, the farmer's son could only pray and work, waiting for God to show him the next step.

God answered John's prayers. Monsieur Melin, the husband of his sister Catherine, told him that Father Balley had opened a school for candidates to the priesthood in Ecully. Madame Vianney went to her husband to plead for John.

"Look, Matthieu," she said, "John can go to Ecully to study with Father Balley. He won't be far from home, and it won't cost a lot because he can stay with his aunt, just as he did when he prepared for his first Communion. Besides, he's seventeen years old now."

Monsieur Vianney gave in at last. "You're right, my dear. If this is what he really wants, I cannot stop him any longer."

Marie Vianney lost no time. She went with her sister, Marguerite, to visit Father Balley. When the tall, thin priest greeted them at the door, the women were struck by the dignity of his manners. Madame Vianney took a deep breath and began to explain the reason for their visit.

"Father Balley," she said, "my son John wants to become a priest. He prays and works very hard. His conduct and example inspire everyone...."

"No," Father Balley interrupted before she could finish. "I cannot take anymore students right now. I am sorry, Madame Vianney."

As they left the parish, Madame Vianney let out a big sigh. "Dear God," she prayed quietly. "Poor John! How can I tell him that he has been turned down? I know what I'll do. First I will speak with Catherine's husband. He will know what to do."

Upon hearing the disappointing news, John's brother-in-law, Monsieur Melin, went to speak directly to Father Balley. Once again, he refused the request.

"At least let him come for an interview, Father Balley," Monsieur Melin insisted. "When you see him, you will change your mind."

"Very well. But I can't promise anything."

Not long after that, John and his mother appeared at the priest's doorstep. *This Madame Vianney is certainly persistent,* Father Balley thought as he opened the door and looked at the young farmer standing before him. John had wavy brown hair, deep-set blue eyes, and was just below medium height.

"Welcome," he said, inviting them both into his rectory. "Now tell me why you want to become a priest, young man."

As they talked, John's sincerity and thoughtful responses began to melt Father Balley's resistance. *Maybe I could squeeze in just one more student,* he found himself thinking. Father Balley was a wise priest and couldn't help noticing how John's face lit up as they talked about the priesthood. He recognized that enthusiasm. He had felt it himself, many years ago. Father Balley asked John a few more questions, but his mind was already made up.

As he walked John and his mother to the door, Father Balley assured John, "Don't worry. I will do whatever I can to help you become a priest."

John could hardly believe it. After waiting so long, it seemed that his dream was going to become a reality!

But leaving behind the farm work he was accustomed to and beginning studies for the priesthood was quite a change for John. He spent mornings and evenings at Father Balley's church, where the classes were conducted. He stayed with his aunt Marguerite, but occasionally walked home to visit his parents in Dardilly.

One evening, John sat at his desk diligently studying Latin. Finally, he closed the book and let out a sigh. He just could not remember all of the Latin verbs and tenses no matter how hard he studied. In those days, Latin was very important. The Mass was said in Latin all over the world, and he had to learn it if he wanted to become a priest.

John closed his eyes and imagined that he was once more at his family farm in Dardilly. He almost laughed when he remembered how he had once thought that farm work was so hard. *Latin is ten times worse!* he thought. His face became serious. *What am I going to do?*

The next day John went to speak to Father Balley. "I think I should go back home," he said in a low voice. "The studies are too difficult for me. I just can't seem to learn Latin and I can't keep up with the other students...."

Father Balley was surprised. Was John really giving up? "If you return home now that will be the end of all your dreams to become a priest. Are you sure you want to do this?"

"No, I'm not sure," said John. "I want to serve God, but I seem to have hit a dead end. I just can't remember all those Latin verbs and tenses, no matter how hard I try."

John felt miserable and wished Father Balley would say something. But Father Balley didn't say a word. Then, suddenly, John had an idea. "I know," he said, talking aloud, but more to himself than to Father Balley. "I'll make a pilgrimage to the shrine of Saint John Francis Régis. I will ask him to pray for me, to help me get through this difficulty."

Father Balley smiled as he watched John leave and walk back up the road toward his aunt's home. *I didn't think he would give up so easily!* he thought.

So John set out on the long trip up the mountains to the holy sanctuary of La Louvesc, where Saint John Francis Régis was honored. The saint had been a great preacher and confessor. When John finally arrived at the shrine, he fell to his knees and begged the great saint to help him get through his studies for the priesthood.

When John finally returned to Ecully, Father Balley was waiting for him. From that time on, the young student began to make just enough progress to continue his studies for the priesthood. He never became a brilliant student, but now he began to hope that his dream would come true. He was always grateful to Saint John Francis Régis for helping him at this critical point in his life. But his difficulties were not over.

4

THE ACCIDENTAL DESERTER

In the autumn of 1809, when John was twenty-three, the Vianney farm received an unexpected visitor. Monsieur Vianney was just coming from the fields when a police officer approached from the road.

"I have something to deliver to John Vianney," announced the officer as he handed a document to Monsieur Vianney.

"What is this all about?" he asked as he looked down in disbelief. "A summons to military service? But isn't he exempt because he is studying to become a priest?"

Madame Vianney, meanwhile, looked out the kitchen window and noticed the police officer talking to her husband. *What could bring the police to our home?* she wondered. Bringing a pitcher of water for her husband and the officer, she was determined to find out. Monsieur Vianney was still reading the summons. He turned to his wife, who was looking over his shoulder, and explained the situation. "There must be some mistake," he concluded.

"We'll just have to ask Father Balley," Madame Vianney replied. She looked just as worried as her husband did.

At that time, Napoleon Bonaparte, the French emperor, was busy waging war with Austria and Spain. He needed more soldiers to maintain his armies. Young men studying for the priesthood were excused from service, however. So why was John drafted?

It was soon discovered that Father Balley had simply forgotten to register John as one of his students for that year. The good priest hurried to Lyons to find out what could be done. But the authorities were unbending. John's name was not on the list of students. It was too late to include him now. They absolutely refused to cancel the summons, and John had no choice but to report for military service.

"John has worked so hard to follow his vocation," lamented Madame Vianney to her husband. "If he goes to war, he might never become a priest."

On October 26, John left Father Balley in Ecully and went to Lyons to report for military service. Just two days later, he fell ill, and the doctor admitted him to the city hospital. He spent two weeks recuperating from a fever. Then he was sent to Roane, where the other recruits had gone ahead to receive military training before leaving for Spain.

John became sick again after making the trip from Lyons to Roane. He ended up in another hospital, and this time he remained for six weeks under the care of the Sisters of Saint Augustine.

It was a cold day in January of 1810. Captain Blanchard sent a messenger to give the young soldier his orders.

"Infantryman Vianney," announced the orderly as he entered John's room. "I've been sent by Captain Blanchard to inform you that you will be leaving tomorrow for Spain with the rest of the regiment."

John was still in the hospital. He was feeling much better, but he was very weak.

Before leaving, the orderly reminded him, "You will need to present yourself at Captain Blanchard's office this afternoon. Don't be late."

Later that day, John set out for the captain's office. On the way, he passed by a church, and he decided to stop in to say a prayer.

I have plenty of time, he said to himself. He knelt before the Blessed Sacrament and poured out his troubles to the Lord. Even though he had no idea what would happen next, John felt peace fill his heart. Not realizing how much time had passed, he suddenly remembered that he had to show up at the captain's office. He quickly started on his way again, but by the time he got to the office it was already closed.

Oh, no, he thought to himself, *what will I do now?* He returned to the hospital.

The next day, January 6, was the feast of the Epiphany. John packed his few belongings and left the hospital, ready for his long journey to Spain.

He was worried about his uncertain future, but he put all his trust in God. He thought about the three Wise Men who came from the East in search of the newborn King of kings. They, too, trusted in God during their long journey.

He said good-bye to the sisters and set off to find his regiment. Once more, he headed toward Captain Blanchard's office. When he arrived, he presented himself to the officer on duty.

"Your detachment has already left. They couldn't wait any longer for you," the soldier stated bluntly.

John stared at him in disbelief. *What else could go wrong?* he thought.

Captain Blanchard stepped forward and frowned at John, who had suddenly turned very white.

"Where have you been? Yesterday you failed to show up and today you are late. I could throw you in jail for this!"

A younger officer spoke up. "Surely, sir, he was not trying to disobey your orders. He just got out of the hospital, and he is here reporting for duty."

The captain didn't carry out his threat, but he told John to catch up with his regiment. The troops were already on their way to Renaison. So the young soldier set out again, on foot and all alone, in the direction of Renaison. He wondered if he could find the others—they had quite a head start, and he wasn't exactly in peak condition for such a long journey. The cold winds made his teeth chatter and sent chills down his back. He pulled out his rosary and began to pray out loud.

By this time, he had entered the mountains of Le Forez. During the summer, the tree-covered mountains were in full bloom, but now everything appeared dreary. Even so, Le Forez was known to be a good place to hide and was a refuge for deserters from the army.

Out of nowhere, a young man with a scraggly beard appeared at John's side and began to ask him questions.

"Who are you? What are you doing here?" Seeing the dumbfounded look on John's face, the mysterious man just shook his head and took John's sack on his own shoulders. He motioned for John to follow behind. They continued climbing up the mountains. John shivered as he struggled to keep up.

"By the way, my name is Guy," the man turned back to smile at his new companion.

"I am John Vianney of Dardilly. I'm on my way to join my regiment in Renaison."

"You don't look like a soldier to me," said Guy, taking note of the pale complexion of the young man.

"That's for sure. But I have my orders."

"Well, if you want, you can join me and many others who are hiding in the forest to avoid military service," Guy replied.

"How could I do that?" John exclaimed. "I can't give up yet. Besides, my parents have already been so worried about me. I don't want to cause them even more anxiety by hiding from the law."

"It's very late, and you must be tired. Just stay here one night, and tomorrow you can be on your way." Guy smiled again and continued his uphill climb.

By this time, John was exhausted. He had barely recovered from his previous illness, and the fever had returned. Cold and miserable, he decided to follow the stranger.

But the following day, John went to look for the mayor of the little village of Les Nöes, Monsieur Paul Fayot. He explained his predicament.

"There's not much you can do about it now," the mayor told him. "You're too late to join your regiment. They already consider you a deserter. If the police find you, you will be arrested. It's not safe for you to continue your journey, so I suggest you stay here with us."

Monsieur Fayot was a simple farmer himself, and he was already hiding two deserters at his farm. Since the time of the Revolution, France had been involved in many wars. Because there was a lot of resistance to the government, desertion was looked upon differently at that time than it would be today. Monsieur Fayot was one of a large group of people who opposed the numerous wars that Napoleon was fighting and saw them as unjust.

"I can find lodging for you," said the mayor. He could see that John was worried. "My cousin, Claudine Fayot, lives close by. She is a widow with four children. To protect yourself, it would be better for you to go by a different name."

Madame Fayot welcomed John, now known as Jérôme Vincent, into her home. She kept his identity a secret and kept him out of view, especially when the police were patrolling in the area.

John kept busy the rest of the winter teaching catechism to Madame Fayot's children and other young people who came to the farmhouse. But he couldn't forget everyone he had left behind.

With the approach of summer, the police began to make surprise appearances in the mountain village. One time, they almost caught John. He was out working when one of the children warned him that the police were in the area. He ran to the stable and hid in the hayloft, covering himself with hay. The police went into the stable and began to search it from top to bottom, stabbing the hay with their swords in order to discover if anyone was hiding there.

John could hardly breathe under the hay, with the heat of the summer sun pounding

John held his breath as the police searched for him....

on the roof. All of a sudden, the point of the policeman's sword pierced him. He nearly screamed, but he managed to stifle his cries. He had never felt pain like that before and silently resolved that he would never complain about anything ever again.

Fortunately, the police did not hurt him seriously; they gave up their search and left him in peace.

God was certainly watching over John. In October of that year, the deserters of Les Nöes received good news. The Emperor Napoleon had defeated Austria and had married the Archduchess Marie-Louise. Now that France was enjoying a period of peace, a general pardon was proclaimed. The pardon extended to all the deserters of the past four years.

John was now safely able to leave the mountains of Le Forez. Madame Fayot and her children cried at his departure. He had become just like one of the family.

Madame Vianney was outside gathering wood for the fire when she caught a glimpse of John trudging up the road to their home. Dropping her bundle, she ran to meet him.

"John, my dear priest," she cried, nearly crushing him in an embrace, "you're home at last!"

John turned just a little red from embarressment. "Yes, mother, I'm finally home," he said. *As for being a priest, I still have a long way to go!* he added silently.

John returned to Dardilly in January of 1811. Shortly after this, on February 8, his mother, whom he loved so much, died at fifty-eight years of age.

5

DON'T GIVE UP

John felt the loss of his mother deeply. She had encouraged him to follow his call to the priesthood from the beginning. His father, however, now understood how important the priesthood was to John. He gave him permission to return to his mentor, Father Balley, who was awaiting John's arrival. Father Balley had prayed daily for John's return, and he had encouraged his parishioners to pray for him, too. In fact, the prayers had multiplied to such an extent that one lady gave a sigh of relief when she saw young Vianney coming down the road.

"Thank heavens that boy is back," she said to her neighbor. "If only he'd hurry up and become a priest! There are plenty of other things I'd like to be praying for, you know!"

John began an intense time of study in preparation for entrance into the Grand Séminaire of Lyons, the next step in his priestly training. Father Balley was a good

9

teacher. He was also a holy priest, and John tried to imitate him. The day came when Father Balley decided that John was ready for the new seminary.

"I know this won't be easy, John, but whatever you do, don't give up!"

The Grand Séminaire of Lyons had been turned into an armory and military hospital during the French Revolution. In 1805, it had been restored as the diocesan seminary. It was a large three-story building with a beautiful garden. Here John found many classmates who were also studying to become priests.

The studies were extremely demanding, however. Everything was taught in Latin, which had always been difficult for John. But he remembered Father Balley's advice and worked as hard as he could. After only a few months, though, it was clear that he was falling far behind the other students. His professors decided that it would be best for John to return home.

"Are you really leaving?" one of the seminarians asked him in disbelief. "It seems so unfair!"

John was shoving his clothes into a trunk. He was returning home that after-noon and really didn't want to talk about it.

"Yes, it's true," he said in a low voice. "I guess God has other plans for me, though I'm not sure what those plans could be." He stuffed the last item into the trunk and the lid closed with a thud. Leaving the Grand Séminaire was the hardest thing John had ever done.

But before he left Lyons, John went to visit one of his friends, Jean Dumond.

"Since it seems that I cannot become a priest, maybe God is calling me to become a brother," he told Jean. Jean, now Brother Gérard, had received the habit of the Brothers of the Petit Collège in Lyons the year before.

"Whatever you do, I'll be praying for you, John," said his friend.

After visiting Brother Gérard, John returned to Ecully. He could finally talk to Father Balley about his great disappointment. Father Balley, of all people, would understand.

"I failed at the seminary. God must not be calling me to the priesthood. Maybe I can become a brother like Brother Gérard. I could join the Brothers at the Petit Collège."

"John," Father Balley spoke firmly, "God has called you to serve him as a priest. I will not rest until you have achieved your goal."

So John took up his textbooks again. With the help of God and Father Balley, he studied with great determination. Three months later, he went to the Grand Séminaire to join the other students taking the examinations for the priesthood.

"John Vianney, you may come in now."

He tried to stay calm as he walked into the examination room. There he found himself face to face with Father Bochard, Vicar General of Lyons, and some of the most educated priests in the diocese. He remembered all the times he had failed in the past and began to panic. When the board of examiners began to question him, John's nervousness got the better of him. The Latin he had studied so hard became jumbled in his mind and his answers were unclear and confused.

"What shall we do about young John Vianney?" the priests asked one another afterward. "We know that Father Balley has done everything to assist him in his studies. He claims that Vianney possesses a good character, that he prays, and that he wants to serve others. It is only the Latin that is holding him back. But we cannot deny that he has failed this examination."

"So, how did it go?" asked Father Balley as soon as John arrived back at the church.

"Well, you see," he replied sadly, "they didn't know quite what to do about me. I didn't pass the examination, but they didn't reject me completely. They said that if I could find a bishop willing to ordain me, I would be free to go to another diocese."

"There's no time to lose," Father Balley said at once. "Tomorrow I will go to Lyons to speak to Father Groboz about your situation. He made it possible for you to receive your first Communion during the Revolution. Now that he is Secretary General for the diocese, he may be able to help you become a priest."

Father Balley went to consult with Father Groboz. The two priests decided to go directly to the office of Father Bochard, who had been present at the examination. They were able to persuade him to give John another chance. Father Bochard decided to go to Ecully himself to see John in his own surroundings.

When Father Bochard and the Superior of the Grand Séminaire arrived at Father Balley's church, John felt more at ease and was able to answer their questions correctly.

The Vicar General, Father Courbon, reviewed John's case. He noted that the young seminarian was devout, prayerful, and had a strong devotion to Mary.

"Yes, he will make a fine priest. God's grace will supply where nature is lacking. I admit him to ordination."

❖ ❖ ❖

"Father Balley! Father Balley!" John was so excited that he wasn't able to maintain his usual calmness. It seemed that all of Ecully had to hear the good news.

"What is it?" Father Balley answered, hurrying over to see what all the commotion was about.

He showed his teacher the letter he had received from Father Courbon.

"I have been accepted!"

On a very hot summer day in August of 1815, John Vianney set out on foot for Grenoble. He carried only a few necessities for the trip, including the alb he would wear for his first Mass. This journey was not like some of the difficult trips he had made in the past. He was so full of joy that the distance of sixty-five miles seemed to disappear beneath his feet.

As he walked, he remembered his dear mother. He could still see her seated in her favorite chair next to a crackling fire. She looked up at him and smiled. "My dear priest," she seemed to be saying to him.

Finally, the town of Grenoble came into view. He could see the church steeple in the distance. His heart skipped a beat. *Tomorrow I will become a priest!*

6

A GOOD FRIEND

I can't believe it finally happened. I am now a priest of God! I am a priest, a priest! John could think of nothing else on his return trip to Ecully and to dear Father Balley. The memory of his ordination and first Mass filled every moment of every hour.

Bishop Simon had made a special trip for the occasion. John was the only candidate for ordination. The bishop smiled and said, "When it comes to ordaining a good priest, it's no trouble at all!"

As John was reliving the events of the past few days, he almost didn't notice that he had reached Father Balley's parish. As usual, Father Balley met him at the door-step. He embraced the new priest and then said, "This time you must give me your blessing, Father Vianney! And then I have good news to give you. The Vicar General has decided that we should have another priest here at the parish to help me. He has appointed you to fill that position!"

"Father Balley, I do not deserve such an honor," said Father Vianney in disbelief. He had never imagined he would be Father Balley's new assistant. This was certainly good news! "I will do everything I can to serve the parish."

❖ ❖ ❖

A few months later, two special guests—Father Bochard and Father Courbon—arrived at the simple parish house of Father Balley and Father Vianney.

"Welcome, welcome, we have been waiting for you," Father Vianney said. He escorted the two priests into the parlor after taking their overcoats.

"Well, well," Father Courbon looked around at the modest surroundings and then at the young priest. "I am interested to see how my new young priest is doing here at Ecully."

"I'm so blessed to be here with Father Balley," said Father Vianney. "And I am learning so much from him. I hope to acquire at least a small part of his virtue."

"Reverend Fathers, you honor us with your presence today," said Father Balley, who had just come into the room. "The cook tells me that dinner is ready. Let us proceed to the dining room."

"This is certainly a feast," said Father Bochard. He helped himself to more potatoes. "Do you manage to eat so well during the weekdays as well?"

Neither Father Balley nor his associate answered at once. *The parishioners must be talking again,* Father Balley thought to himself. They were of the opinion that the priests of Ecully did far too much penance. They didn't give up food they liked just during Lent, but all the time. Both Father Balley and Father Vianney understood that penance can help us remember the importance of our relationship with God.

"Well, our daily meals are not quite as fancy as this, you see. We are just two simple priests accustomed to country living," Father Balley smiled, and the wrinkles on his face made him look much older than he actually was.

"It's interesting how people in a small village will talk, isn't it?" Father Courbon was looking right at Father Vianney. "Well, you know what I tell them—I say that they should be thanking God to have such fine priests who aren't afraid to make a few sacrifices. Just make sure you take care of your health, too—or we won't have any priests for the parish!"

"The people here are very pleased with Father Vianney," Father Balley commented. "They only wish that he had permission to hear confessions. People would be lining up outside his confessional."

Father Vianney's face turned beet red.

"Indeed, is that so?" Father Courbon looked at Father Vianney again. "We will have to see about that...."

All of a sudden, the conversation was interrupted by a knock at the door. Father Balley got up to answer the door and returned a few moments later with an unexpected guest. To Father Vianney's surprise, Madame Fayot, the widow who had helped him when he became separated from his regiment during the war, entered the room. She recognized her beloved "son" at once and went over to greet him.

"My dear child," she cried out, "I'm so happy to see you again!"

Madame Fayot's arrival created a distraction and Father Vianney was grateful for the chance to change the subject!

❖ ❖ ❖

The days and months passed quickly. Time was running out for Father Balley, who had lived through the terrors and hardships of the Revolution. During 1817, his health continued to decline. An ulcer developed in his leg, and he had to remain in bed. His devoted assistant took over most of his duties in the parish.

One day in December, Father Balley called Father Vianney to his bedside. "Well, my son, my time to meet the Lord is soon approaching. I would like to receive the last rites now...."

"Yes, Father," he whispered, trying to hide his tears. "There are some people waiting outside. They were hoping to receive your blessing. Can they come in?"

Father Balley nodded, and then he grasped Father Vianney's hand. "Now it is up to you, to carry on...."

After the parishioners had left and the two priests were alone again, Father Balley said good-bye to his young friend and asked for his prayers. Then the holy priest breathed his last, like a flickering candle that has come to the end of its wick. Father Vianney had loved him like a father and would never forget him.

After Father Balley's death, another priest, Father Tripier, was assigned to be the new pastor of Ecully. He was very different from the former pastor. He didn't approve of Father Vianney's strict lifestyle and worn-out cassock. The parishioners knew that Father Vianney was extremely generous with his possessions. It was no wonder, then, that the young priest often went around in threadbare clothes. But Father Tripier didn't see things in quite the same way.

In February of 1818, Father Vianney went to see Father Courbon, the Vicar General.

"Father Vianney," Father Courbon looked directly at him with his frank yet kindly gaze. "The Lord is calling you to serve him in Ars. The last pastor of this small village died only a few weeks after his arrival. The people of Ars need someone to teach them about God's love. You will find people who need you there."

"I am ready to go," Father Vianney answered at once. Yes, to bring people to God, he was ready for anything.

7

DOES ANYONE KNOW THE WAY TO ARS?

"What should we do now, Father?" Madame Bibost, his friend from Ecully, sighed as she tried to see through the heavy mist that had settled on the plain.

"Well, it's not the first time I've been lost," Father Vianney chuckled. Madame Bibost was accompanying the new pastor, or Curé, to his parish in Ars. During Father Vianney's years in Ecully, Madame Bibost had often checked in on Father Balley and his young assistant. Every once in a while, they needed help with the finer details of housekeeping. *He still can't wash his own clothes properly*, she silently lamented. Her motherly heart wouldn't be at ease until she saw him safely settled in at his new parish.

Father Vianney and Madame Bibost journeyed on foot, followed by a cart carrying his few possessions. There were no forests or hills to breathe life into the dreary landscape. The road stretched out beneath their feet with occasional birch and oak trees scattered along the way. The journey from Ecully to Ars was nearly nineteen miles.

Holding up his lantern, Father Vianney caught sight of something moving in the distance. "Let's go that way," he turned to Madame Bibost. "I see something ahead."

When they got closer, Madame Bibost called out, "Look, there are some children leading their flocks of sheep."

"We're trying to find the road to Ars," Father Vianney told them. "Do you know where it is?"

The young shepherds looked at the priest quizzically, but they didn't say anything. Trying to keep themselves warm, they rubbed their mittens together and stamped their feet.

"Do you know the way to Ars?" Father Vianney asked again. When he saw the blank looks on their faces, he realized that they only spoke their own local dialect. In that particular region of the country, the people spoke the French language with different vocabulary and grammar. So he began to make hand motions and then said a few times, "Ars...Ars...the road to Ars."

Finally, one of the children nodded and pointed him in the right direction.

One of the children pointed out the road to Ars.

"Thank you, my son," Father Vianney smiled at him. "You have shown me the way to Ars. I will show you the way to heaven."

The boy indicated that they were standing at the boundary lines of the parish. Father Vianney knelt down on the spot, and he began to pray for his new flock. Then he got up and began walking with renewed energy. His parish was waiting for him.

At that time, most French people probably hadn't even heard of Ars. It was a forgotten village in a distant corner of the country, close to France's eastern border. When the town came into view, Father Vianney saw about forty clay houses in between the trees. The church was a simple, yellowish building with a small rectory close by. The roads were in very poor condition. This helped to keep strangers out and the townspeople at home. The sight of Ars certainly didn't offer much encouragement to its new pastor.

"It's not much to look at," he whispered softly, "but one day this parish won't be able to hold the crowds of people who will come here." Then he continued on his way.

Little did the townspeople of Ars suspect that these words of Father Vianney would soon be fulfilled.

❖ ❖ ❖

When the church bell rang for Mass the next morning, the villagers realized that they had a new pastor. Some of them received the news with joy, but most of the people didn't pay much attention. What difference could a new priest make in Ars?

On Sunday, February 13, Father Vianney was installed as the new Curé. After receiving the stole symbolizing his authority as pastor, he spoke to his parishioners for the first time. Then he celebrated Mass. Afterward, the parishioners streamed out of the church, talking among themselves.

"What did you think of our new pastor, Madame?" a young mother asked one of the older ladies of the parish.

"Bit of a young whippersnapper, if you ask me," she replied with a twinkle in her eye. "But he seems bound and determined to make a good start as pastor here in Ars."

"I hope he lasts longer than the last priest!" laughed a young man as he walked by.

"Impertinent young fellow," the older lady muttered under her breath. Aloud, she added to her companion, "I have a feeling, though, that there's more to this young pastor than meets the eye. I think we have a holy priest in our parish."

And the two women were on their way.

Two weeks after his installation as Curé, Madame Bibost traveled to Dardilly so that she could accompany Marguerite, Father Vianney's sister, to Ars.

"John!" Marguerite cried out happily when she arrived and Father Vianney greeted them. "I've finally made it. What a trip it was! Thank goodness for Madame Bibost. I would never have gotten here without her."

"Come in, come in," the amiable priest said, welcoming the two ladies into his small parish house. "It's so wonderful to see you, Marguerite. I've missed everyone at home so much."

"Well, you're in luck," she said with a smile. "I have so much news to share with you!"

Marguerite looked around the house. On the ground floor there were two rooms, the kitchen and the dining room. A wealthy lady, Mademoiselle d'Ars, had provided many fine pieces of furniture and other objects for the rectory. But Father Vianney preferred simple things for himself. He had asked that the fancy furniture he didn't need be removed by Mademoiselle d'Ars. He had already given away his mattress to someone who needed it, while he slept on boards in the attic.

"Oh, dear," Father announced to his guests, "I'm sorry, but I have nothing to offer you to eat. Wait, let me see. I do have a few potatoes that I cooked." He brought them out cheerfully. "They're still quite good."

Marguerite and Madame Bibost both looked at the potatoes, cooked a few days before, and then at each other.

"No thank you, John," said Marguerite, trying not to look at the soggy plateful of potatoes her brother was offering her. "It's far too early to eat anything."

"But surely you must be hungry. How about you, Madame Bibost? You traveled so far," said Father Vianney.

"I think I could really use a glass of water, Father," she replied, stifling a laugh.

Father Vianney hurried back into the kitchen and brought out a pitcher of water and two glasses for the ladies.

"Well, I need to go over to the church now. Please make yourselves at home, and I'll be back later."

When Father Vianney was safely outside, Madame Bibost turned to Marguerite. "I'll check in the kitchen to see if we can prepare something fresh for supper. It does not look as if your brother has had a good meal since I left him here," Madame Bibost said.

"Oh, look," Marguerite said as she glanced out the window. "I think we'll have a fine meal indeed. Would you like to help me catch some pigeons for our dinner?"

Later on, Father Vianney left the church and walked down the path leading to the parish house. He noticed the delicious aroma wafting from the kitchen window.

"My goodness!" he exclaimed when he saw the roasted birds on the serving platter. "What are these? Not the poor pigeons? I admit they were a little annoying, but I was just starting to get used to them. Everything does smell delicious, though. This will be a treat indeed!"

When it was time to leave, Marguerite told her brother, "Promise me that you'll take care of yourself, John."

"Gothon, don't worry about me," Father Vianney smiled at his sister. "I'm fine here. But you had better pray for my parishioners."

Father Vianney put his whole heart and soul into his ministry. Even though it was a small parish, he kept very busy. Early each morning, he arose and went to the church. There he spent many hours in prayer, speaking with God and praying especially for people who had not yet discovered God's love for them. At times, he also prayed outdoors, enjoying the beauty of nature. He often followed the path of the Fontblin, a narrow stream leading to the shade of majestic oak trees.

In the afternoons, he made visits to the families of Ars. Little by little, the villagers began to realize how fortunate they were to have such a dedicated pastor in their village.

8

THE NEW CURÉ BEGINS
HIS WORK

Father Vianney paced back and forth. He had long since forgotten the time. It must have been well past midnight. He could barely keep his eyes open. Clutching his papers tightly, he went over the text again and again.

He wanted to commit everything to memory. Soon it would be Sunday morning, and he would have to deliver his sermon to the parishioners. In the beginning, this was how the Curé prepared for Sunday Mass each week. He wanted to preach sermons that the people of Ars wouldn't forget.

This particular Sunday, Father Vianney was determined not to forget anything. He remembered what had happened only the Sunday before. Right in the middle of his sermon, his mind had gone blank. Completely embarrassed, he had had to leave the pulpit.

During Father's sermons, some of the people yawned and some actually fell asleep. Others were more concerned about what their neighbors were wearing and looked in every direction *except* the pulpit.

When he got up to speak this time, however, the words just seemed to flow from his mouth. He put his whole heart into his sermon, encouraging his parishioners to let go of many bad habits that were harming their families and their town. There was total silence in the church as he spoke. No one laughed or whispered this time.

After Mass, Mademoiselle d'Ars went into the sacristy to talk to Father Vianney. He was holding his head in his hands, deep in prayer. The lady of the manor waited respectfully for a few minutes. She was known for her religious devotion and care for the sick.

"Mademoiselle," Father Vianney said as he went to greet her, "it's always a pleasure to see you at Mass. I am grateful for all your support. I hope there is nothing wrong."

"Monsieur le Curé," she replied, "thank you. I am well. But I'm concerned about you. You delivered your sermon with great energy this week, but you seem dreadfully tired. You must take care of yourself."

"Mademoiselle," the priest shook his head sadly, "how can I rest when I see the condition my parish is in? Only a few people come to Mass. Many spend the Lord's Day working. When they finish their work in the fields, they go to the bars in town instead of spending time with their families."

"Yes, you're right," Mademoiselle d'Ars sighed. "But you must understand it wasn't always like this in Ars. Before the Revolution, faith was a part of daily life. But then the Reign of Terror came, and the church was turned into a club where the citizens gathered for meetings. Good priests went into hiding and were only able to make occasional visits to Ars.

"By the time the Church was free to open her doors again, many people had fallen away from the practice of their religion. Now that you are here, however, we are hopeful that our town will return to God and the Church."

"It won't be because of me," Father Vianney said firmly. "Only the great mercy and love of God can bring about such a conversion. I cannot rest until it is accomplished. But I shouldn't weigh you down with all my concerns. I must thank you for these beautiful vestments. You and your brother, the Vicomte Françoise, have overwhelmed me with your generosity."

"I see that you have already made improvements in the church," remarked Mademoiselle d'Ars.

Father Vianney might not have been very particular when it came to his own clothes and furniture, but the parish church was to be a place of beauty for the entire town. He had already purchased a new altar with his own money. He put angel statues on either side of the tabernacle. A fresh coat of paint brightened the dull woodwork around the altar.

"I have more plans for the church." The Curé seemed to forget his other troubles when he talked about the church. "I would like to construct a new bell tower and also add some side chapels dedicated to our Lady and other saints."

"Yes, and you must let me contribute to these worthy causes. But I am keeping you—isn't the catechism class supposed to begin now?" Mademoiselle d'Ars asked.

Father Vianney considered his catechism classes a very important part of his ministry at Ars. He usually gathered the children together at one o'clock on Sunday afternoons. He would use various methods to get them to come on time. "The first one to arrive will get a prayer card!" he would tell them.

"Why yes! My apologies, Mademoiselle, I mustn't be late. We shall talk more of this another day." And with that, he hurried away.

9

REBUILDING HIS CHURCH

One day Father Vianney went to look for the fiddler who would be playing the music for the village dance that evening.

"My good man," the Curé said kindly, "how much do they usually pay you for playing your fiddle?"

When the fiddler told him, the priest handed him twice that amount of money.

The fiddler gave Father Vianney a knowing smile. "I see what's going on here, Monsieur le Curé. The pastors in the other villages don't approve of these dances, either. Say they cause trouble." The fiddler stuffed the coins into his pocket. "Well, I guess there won't be any dancing in Ars tonight! Too bad, I learned a new tune just for the occasion. Can't say I'm sorry to go home with extra money in my pocket, though."

Although dancing to the tune of a fiddle sounds fairly tame nowadays, all those dances were giving Ars a rather questionable reputation by eighteenth-century standards. Among neighboring villages, Ars was known as the place to party, and this concerned Father Vianney. He hoped to help the young people of his parish make responsible decisions and find better ways to spend their free time.

The Curé also saw that many people in Ars struggled with drinking problems. Sometimes they spent all their wages at the local taverns. Many families in Ars were suffering as a consequence. Eventually, Father Vianney managed to have the two bars that were near the church closed down.

Nothing happened overnight. But little by little, the people of Ars began to notice a change in their village.

❖ ❖ ❖

One Sunday during the summer months, while the cut corn was still on the ground, a farmer came up to Father Vianney before Mass.

"Monsieur le Curé," he began, "our crops are in danger. The sky is becoming dark, and it could start raining at any moment. Shouldn't we make an exception and go to the fields today?"

Father Vianney understood all too well what could happen if the storms washed everything away. Growing up on a farm, he had worked long days in the fields. But it had taken long and patient work to cultivate renewed honor for the Lord's Day in his parish. He was reluctant to begin making exceptions....

"I will pray about this," the Curé reassured the farmer.

During his sermon, Father Vianney told the people not to worry because the weather would be fine. The promise of the Curé came true! The storm passed them by, and they had good weather for the next two weeks.

Father Vianney was rebuilding his church spiritually by helping many people begin to put their faith into action again. But he was also restoring the church physically. In 1820, he went ahead with his plans for the construction of a new bell tower. He also had special side chapels dedicated to our Lady and to his Confirmation patron, Saint John the Baptist. Later, Father Vianney added other chapels to the church. In 1837, he dedicated one to Saint Philomena. She was an early Christian martyr, but no one knew about her until 1802, when a workman discovered her tomb in the ancient Catacomb of Saint Priscilla in Rome. Saint

Philomena quickly made up for lost time. As people learned about her, miracles started to multiply through her intercession. Saint Philomena became Father Vianney's guide, intercessor, and special friend in heaven.

10

HOUSE OF PROVIDENCE

Just as Father Vianney began to make headway in his little parish, however, he met new challenges. There were some parishioners who resented the changes happening in Ars. Some felt that their new pastor was making life too hard for them. They weren't interested in living their faith more deeply or honoring the Lord's Day. They even went so far as to try to drive him away.

Father Vianney admitted to a friend, "If I had known how difficult things would be, I would have been scared to death."

The Curé didn't limit his pastoral care to the parish of Ars, however. He also traveled to the surrounding parishes to preach and hear confessions. People came in great numbers to listen to him. So many people went to confession when he was at Trévoux that they almost knocked over the confessional!

Father Vianney occasionally visited the neighboring villages to help out with baptisms, marriages, and funerals. One rainy day in October, he made the trip on foot to the neighboring town of Rancé to hear the confession of a sick man. By the time he arrived, he was soaking wet. He felt so sick that he lay down on the floor by the bed of the sick man and heard his confession.

"I was more ill than he was," the Curé mentioned to one of his parishioners the following day.

Back at Ars, he never lost a moment. He was ahead of his time in seeing the importance of establishing a school for the girls of Ars. In 1823, after much prayer and reflection, he chose two farm girls, Catherine Lassagne and Benoît Lardet, to oversee and teach at the new school. Since they had no experience, he sent them to study with the Sisters of Saint Joseph in Fareins. Catherine and Benoît left behind their life on the farm and began to prepare for their future role as teachers.

The school for girls officially opened in November of 1824 and was called La Providence. Then the Curé had the inspiration to take in homeless orphans who had nowhere to go. Soon the house was full of children. There were times when Catherine didn't know if they would have enough food to feed everyone. They didn't charge any tuition for the school, so there were always financial problems. At one point, they were caring for sixty children.

One day, the Curé happened to meet a little girl who had no family or home. He brought her to La Providence.

"The good God has sent us another child to care for," he told Catherine.

"Monsieur le Curé, we don't have any empty beds!" exclaimed Catherine. "Where will we put her?"

"We can't turn her away. Where will she go? What will become of her?" answered the priest.

Catherine sighed. She knew she wasn't going to win this argument. "Yes, Father, you're right," she agreed. "We don't have much, but somehow we will share it with this little one."

As Catherine led the new child inside, she thought, *It's certainly not always easy working with a saint!*

11

A WHOLE NEW ARS

It was almost evening. Father Vianney couldn't help but notice the beauty of creation as the sun turned into a ball of fire and sent streaks of color across the sky. Lost in thought, he walked down the path to the church. One of the village farmers had left his hoe near the door and was sitting quiet-ly in one of the pews. It was almost dark inside, except for the flicker of candles. Father Vianney remembered how one of the villagers had explained his favorite way of praying.

"I look at the good God—and God looks at me," the priest repeated thoughtfully to himself.

After a few moments, Father Vianney quietly slipped outside again. His heart was light. It was so wonderful to see the people of the parish stop to pray in the church as this farmer had done. As he walked back to the rectory, Father Vianney smiled as he saw other villagers passing by with their carts. Back in his house, Father Vianney finished off a letter to a friend. "I am in good parish

—it may be small, but the people serve God with all their hearts," he wrote.

The church bells began to ring. From his desk, he could see families coming out of their homes and heading to the church for evening prayers.

What a difference, thought Father Vianney as he prepared to return to the church for the service, *compared to when I first arrived here!*

Remarkable changes were happening on Sundays, too. When the Curé celebrated Mass, the people filled the pews.

Visitors to Ars noticed a special peace there. The villagers were hospitable and friendly to travelers and eager to help anyone in trouble. When visitors returned to their own cities and towns, they realized what a difference it makes when people care for one another.

Of course, the change in Ars didn't mean Father Vianney's work got much easier! One night, when Father Vianney had returned home for the evening, he heard someone pounding insistently on the gate outside. He was tired and didn't want to go down to see who was there right away. But the pounding continued to grow louder and louder.

"Well, I won't get any rest tonight until I see what is going on out there," he muttered to himself as he grabbed his lighted candle and went down the stairs leading to the ground floor.

When he opened the door, he saw a man waiting anxiously with his horse and cart close by.

"What can I do for you, my good man?" the Curé asked.

"Please, Monsieur le Curé," the man answered. "I would like to go to confession—tonight!"

Father Vianney smiled. *So much for a peaceful evening,* he thought. *I cannot refuse this man.* Then, stifling a chuckle, he added under his breath, *Having holy parishioners is not as simple as it sounds!* And he welcomed the man inside.

❖ ❖ ❖

News about the saintly Curé of Ars was beginning to spread to other towns and villages. The people of Dardilly, Ecully, and Les Noës remembered him well, and they traveled willingly to see him. Others had heard so much about him and wanted to find out the truth for themselves. Some people were just curious, while a good many believed him to be a saint.

Father Vianney's love for God and for people had a way of getting through even to people who had no interest in changing their lives. But the Curé of Ars remained humble, and kept his sense of humor.

After Mass one day, one of the men of the village remarked, "You're becoming quite the celebrity, Father. All these visitors coming to Ars!"

To the man's surprise, Father Vianney burst out laughing.

"Funny you should say that. You know, today I received two letters," he said. "One person wrote to tell me that I am a great saint. The other person wrote to say that he thinks I'm a fake. The first letter didn't make me any better than I really am—and the second didn't make me any worse!"

As the crowds of pilgrims poured into Ars, Catherine remarked, "Monsieur le Curé, there are missionaries who go to the ends of the earth to bring people to God. But here, people chase after you!"

12

THE GRAPPIN STRIKES BACK

Amid all the good things that were happening in Ars, Father Vianney began to notice strange things happening at the rectory. Not sure what was going on, he decided to ask André, a young man who lived in the village, for help.

"I've been hearing loud noises at night. I don't know what it can be—maybe it's an animal. Or it could be burglars, though I haven't seen anyone. Would you mind staying over one night to help me find out what's making all these unusual noises?"

"Sure, Monsieur le Curé," replied André. "Do you mind if I bring my hunting gun along, just in case? We may need to defend ourselves."

That evening, André stayed at the rectory. At first, everything seemed fine. Sitting by the fire, he talked with Father Vianney until late into the night. But afterward, André wasn't able to sleep. All alone in the dark, he began to feel nervous. *I'm just imagining things. Nobody else is here.*

All of a sudden, the front door started rattling and loud blows banged against the walls. André grabbed his gun and ran to the window. There was nobody there. The Curé had also come out of his room at the sound of the noise.

"Did you hear that, too?"

"Of course I did," replied the young man. He tried to steady himself, but his legs were shaking beneath him.

"What do you think it could be?" asked the priest.

André hadn't seen anything at all that could have caused so much commotion.

"It seemed like the devil himself," he replied.

After a while the disturbance stopped, and everything was peaceful again. In the morning, though, when the Curé asked André to stay for another night, he refused.

"Sorry, Monsieur le Curé, I think I've had enough. Keeping watch for burglars is one thing. Sleeping in a haunted house is another!"

Father Vianney understood. He was starting to feel the same way. So he asked other men of the town to keep him company and be on the lookout for troublemak-

"Did you hear that, too?"

ers. One after another, they bravely volunteered to help him. And one after another, like André, they politely refused to spend another night listening to the spooky noises in Father Vianney's home. The disturbances took on various forms—loud talking, curtains shaking, chairs turning over. At other times, they could hear bats flapping their wings, or bees swarming in his bedroom, or horses galloping in the dining room.

"I finally realized that it must be the devil," he told Bishop Devie later on. "I was afraid—so it certainly didn't come from God."

Although he felt afraid, Father Vianney realized he didn't need his bodyguards anymore. Whenever he heard strange noises in the house, he would pray. Then he began to notice a pattern. The frightening noises always seemed to happen right before someone would decide to try to live a more Christian life. Very often someone would come to Father Vianney the next day and ask to go to confession. They wanted to be reconciled with God.

Once, the Curé of Ars was invited to preach at the parish in Saint-Trivier-sur-Moignans in the middle of winter. While he was staying at the rectory, the other priests in the house began to hear the same strange noises at night.

"Father Vianney," they asked him the next morning, "what were you doing? You kept us awake all night long!"

"It was the Grappin," he explained. That was his nickname for the devil. "He's pretty angry because so much good is happening during this mission."

"How can you be sure it is the devil?" one the priests, Father Chevalon, asked. "Maybe it was only the wind outside that caused the noise last night."

The very next night, they all awoke to a terrible banging and uproar. It felt like an earthquake shaking the foundations of the house. The pastor of Saint-Trivier, Father Grangier, ran down the hallway toward Father Vianney's room.

"Someone must be murdering the Curé of Ars!" yelled out Father Benoît.

Everyone headed to his room, expecting the worst. When they opened the door, however, Father Vianney looked up from under the covers sheepishly. *It's bad enough in my own home*, he thought. *Must these noises really follow me wherever I go?*

"Don't worry. It was the Grappin," he apologized. "I'm sorry to have caused you any inconvenience. He is probably angry because there will be a big fish to catch tomorrow."

For the Curé of Ars, a "big fish" was someone who wanted to be reconciled to God after a long time of sinful behavior. The other priests were still unsure about his explanation. The next day, they kept an eye out to see if any "big fish" showed up for the sacrament of Penance.

Sure enough, the following day one of the townspeople who had not come to church in many years asked Father Vianney to hear his confession.

That certainly was a big fish, thought Father Chevalon. Father Chevalon had been a soldier of the Republic and then a mission-ary for the Church and had seen many things in his lifetime. But he had no expla-nation for the mysterious events happening since Father Vianney had come to their parish.

That priest is a saint, he said to himself. *I will never make fun of him again.*

These battles with the devil went on for years. But the devil admitted defeat in the end. Gradually, the attacks decreased until finally the Curé was left in peace.

13

FLIGHT AND RETURN TO ARS

Louise Martin and her grandmother set out to visit the holy Curé in April of 1843. Louise was a fun-loving eighteen-year-old, but she had a generous heart. For the past few months, she had felt a call to the religious life. Her parents weren't very happy about this, so she turned to her grandmother for help.

"How can I be sure that God is calling me? Will the Curé be able to give me an answer?" she asked her grandmother as they traveled to Ars.

"I am sure he'll be able to help you understand what God may be calling you to. The Curé is a saint. They say he hears confessions as long as eighteen hours a day. Hundreds of pilgrims arrive in Ars every day."

"Oh, I hope he can help me," Louise sighed. She thought about her parents. She hadn't told them about her trip to Ars. If God was calling her to be a sister, how could she help them to understand?

When they arrived in Ars, Louise was amazed to see huge crowds of people everywhere. There were gentlemen and ladies of noble background as well as peasants and merchants from the farms and cities. They came by train, by cart, by carriage, by river, and by foot. The railway station issued tickets to Ars for eight days because that's how long it would take to see the Curé. Some people camped out in the meadows because there was no room for them to stay in town.

"How long do you think we will wait to see the Curé, Grandmother?" Louise asked.

"I don't know, my dear," her grandmother replied. "I've heard that sometimes the Curé comes out and calls a person who is sick or cannot wait long. He doesn't know the people, but it seems he has a special gift of knowledge from God."

"I've heard that too," said Louise. "Just yesterday someone told me that the mother of a large family was standing in line. Father Vianney went up to her and told her that she could go to confession before the others. He knew that she couldn't wait much longer."

After a long wait, it was finally Louise's turn to go to confession. But at that very moment, Father Vianney came out. All eyes turned in the direction of the frail priest as he walked quickly toward the sacristy to prepare to celebrate the Eucharist.

No! thought Louise. *I can't miss my chance, not after waiting so long!* She summoned her courage and ran after him.

"Monsieur le Curé," she called out, "I would like to go to confession before I receive Communion at Mass today."

"You're not very shy, are you?" he asked with a twinkle in his eye as the mob pressed around him.

"No, not really." Now she was just a little embarrassed that she had run after the Curé.

"All right, then, I can hear your confession right now."

"Here?" Louise looked around uncertainly. *Here goes nothing!* she thought, and knelt down on the dusty ground.

After receiving absolution, Louise told the Curé about her desire to be consecrated to God and become a sister.

"Yes, I think your vocation is from God," answered the priest gently. "There's no reason for you to put it off."

When she returned home, Louise explained everything that had happened in Ars to her parents. Soon after, she entered the Visitation Order and took a new name, Sister Marie Anastasie.

❖ ❖ ❖

There are many saints we call "martyrs" because they gave up their lives in order to be faithful to God. Father Vianney could be considered a martyr for the sacrament of Reconciliation.

After only a couple hours of sleep, he would get up very early and start hearing confessions an hour later. The confessional in his parish church was a very small enclosed space, which became very hot in the summer. In the winter an icy wind blew down from the mountains.

It was difficult to heat the church well, and Father's feet would become numb with cold as he sat there hour after hour. When he left the church, the pilgrims to Ars followed him.

He did discover ways around the constant attention, though. When he went to his house, sometimes he would toss a handful of religious medals into the crowd. The crowd was always delighted—a medal from the hands of the holy Curé was a special reminder of the pilgrimage to Ars! While everyone dashed to pick them up, Father Vianney would sneak inside and lock the door behind him.

Although he was willing to work very hard and make many sacrifices for the sake of his parishioners and the visitors to Ars, Father Vianney also began to wish he could spend more time in prayer.

Perhaps it is time that I leave this parish to the care of another, he thought. *It is a great responsibility to be a pastor. I have seen so many people leave their sins behind here in Ars, but heaven knows I have many sins of my own that I want to do penance for.* Father Vianney expressed his desires to his bishop, but the bishop didn't want him to leave.

On May 3, a few days after Louise Martin's visit, the Curé became very ill. He was leading the May devotions in honor of Mary in the church when suddenly he began to choke.

Helpers rushed to his side. They carried him to a nearby room. Dr. Saunier arrived quickly and diagnosed the illness as a serious case of pneumonia.

Meanwhile, the parishioners and pilgrims gathered around the altar of Father Vianney's favorite saint, Philomena, begging for a cure for their dear priest. As he lay dying, Father Vianney promised that he would have a hundred Masses said in honor of Saint Philomena. Then he fell into a coma. He didn't speak or open his eyes.

*Hundreds of pilgrims came to Ars every day
to see Father Vianney.*

Dr. Saunier believed the end was near. Checking the sick man's pulse, he said softly, "He doesn't have much time left."

Somehow Father Vianney was able to understand what the doctor was saying. In the depths of his soul, he prayed, "My God, I have only begun to serve you and your people! Mary, my mother, and Saint Philomena, my friend, pray for me."

All at once he opened his eyes and began to talk. By the next morning, he was well again. But a new fear struck the town of Ars. Now that the Curé was healed, would he remain in Ars, or would he go somewhere else to find the peace and quiet and time to pray that he wanted so much?

The bishop agreed that Father Vianney should take some time for rest. Father Raymond from a neighboring parish in Savigneux had been spending a great deal of time in Ars. He was willing to take the Curé's place while he was away.

Father Raymond actually had secret ambitions of his own. He dreamed of becoming the pastor of Ars. He already had plans to organize and manage the pilgrimages. *After all,* he thought to himself, *I could do an even better job than Father Vianney is doing.*

In September, Father Vianney related his plans to the young priest.

"Father Raymond, I am going to visit my brother François in Dardilly. I am entrusting to you an important letter I've written to the bishop. I hope he will finally allow me to move somewhere so I can devote myself to prayer...."

"Don't worry, Monsieur le Curé, I'll take care of everything while you are gone."

"I plan to leave this evening, but don't tell anyone. I want to be on my way without anyone else knowing."

"Of course."

Somehow, though, the news got out. When Father Vianney attempted to leave Ars after midnight, villagers were waiting to stop him. But he kept right on going.

Jean Pertinand, the schoolmaster of Ars, followed him along the way.

"Monsieur le Curé," he called out, "why are you leaving us?"

"I have asked to retire. In Dardilly, I will await the bishop's answer."

It was a dark night, and the Curé became lost in the fields. Fortunately, Jean Pertinand was still following Father Vianney, trying to convince him to remain in Ars. He realized they had begun to walk in circles.

"Father, haven't we seen all this before?" he laughed. "If I can't convince you to stay, at least let me take you to Dardilly."

The next morning, all of Ars found out that their beloved pastor was gone. The schoolgirls at La Providence were crying. The pilgrims didn't know what to do. So they decided to follow Father Vianney to Dardilly.

The church at Ars was empty now. Father Raymond soon realized that there would be no pilgrimages to organize without Father Vianney.

When the Curé saw hundreds of pilgrims arriving in Dardilly, he understood how much people were counting on him.

What was I thinking? My parishioners still want me to guide them. Maybe God is calling me to stay in Ars and continue the work I have begun....

The bishop had offered him another parish, but Father Vianney decided to go back to Ars. He had been away only eight days, but the bells rang out and everyone rejoiced when he returned. The farmers left the fields and joined the pilgrims gathered to welcome back their priest.

Father Vianney felt a new peace as he greeted the people. Now he understood that

God still wanted him to serve at the parish in Ars. "My children," he exclaimed, "I have returned! I will never leave you again!"

14

PROPHECIES, MIRACLES,
AND VISIONS

François Dorel was a carefree young man from another town. In 1852, he agreed to accompany a friend to Ars.

"This priest hears confessions day and night and works miracles too. I'd like to see him," his friend said.

"Well, I'll go along," said François. "But I'd rather go hunting while we're there. I'll take my dog and my gun. You can go to confession if you like."

As the travelers entered the town, the Curé happened to be passing by. He was blessing the people, but he paused to look at François and his dog.

"Monsieur," the Curé said seriously, "if only your soul could be as beautiful as your dog!"

François' face turned bright red. His dog was always so eager to please him, and he followed François everywhere. *This dog has been far more faithful to me than I have been to God.* He decided to go to confession to the Curé. The priest encouraged him to spend his life in service to God and others. François took his advice and later became a religious brother.

Father Raymond remained in Ars from 1845 to 1853 as Father Vianney's assistant. The bishop then assigned Father Toccanier to be the Curé's assistant. He remained in Ars for the rest of the saintly priest's life and witnessed many of the miraculous happenings going on at that time.

One evening, Father Toccanier was talking with the Curé. Father Vianney told him, "I was so embarrassed today; I didn't know what to do."

"What happened?"

"A lady came with a child who had a big tumor under his eye. She grabbed my hand and touched it to the tumor. It disappeared immediately."

Father Vianney might have felt surprised, but Father Toccanier was not. "This time you cannot say that Saint Philomena worked the miracle, Monsieur le Curé," he pointed out.

"Oh, I think she still had something to do with it," answered Father Vianney. He never took credit for the many miracles and conversions taking place in Ars. He told the people it was Saint Philomena's prayers that had obtained the desired cure. When he hoped that someone would change their sinful behavior, he turned to the Blessed Mother for help.

Besides the many miracles and healings taking place, the Curé of Ars received other special favors from God. He didn't like to talk about these gifts, but other people noticed and spoke about them. One such person was Mademoiselle Êtiennette Durié. She was very trustworthy and had helped to collect donations for Father Vianney's charitable causes. One day she came to Ars to deliver an especially large donation.

Mademoiselle Durié arrived at the rectory in the afternoon. Catherine Lassagne welcomed her and told her that the Curé was in the other room. Mademoiselle Durié could hear voices as she approached the door. Who could the Curé be talking to?

"What do you ask of me?" a sweet voice was saying.

"My Mother, I pray that people may be reconciled with God. I also pray for the health of many sick people who have asked for prayers—especially for one person who has suffered for a long time."

"She will be cured, but not right away."

They must be talking about me, thought Mademoiselle Durié. She had been stricken with cancer, and she knew the Curé had been praying for her.

Entering the room, she gasped and stifled a cry. A beautiful lady was standing in front of the fireplace. She was clothed in bright white robes and had a crown of brilliant stars on her head. She was so radiant that Mademoiselle Durié could hardly bear to look at her. The beautiful lady smiled at her, and then she was gone.

Mademoiselle Durié blinked her eyes and looked around. Father Vianney was so still and quiet that she was afraid he was dead. She didn't want to startle him, so she tugged at his cassock.

"Dear God, could it be you?" he asked.

"No, Monsieur le Curé, it's just me."

Startled, Father Vianney turned and saw Mademoiselle Durié standing next to him. When she told him about the vision, he asked her not to tell anyone about it. A few months later, on August 15, the feast day when we celebrate Mary being taken up into heaven, Mademoiselle Durié was cured of her disease.

15

LAST DAYS OF THE CURÉ

In the last years of his life, Father Vianney had the support of faithful friends. He was in his seventies, and his health was not always good. Catherine Lassagne was on hand to look out for her spiritual father. At times, she had to insist that he have something to eat.

Father Toccanier was like a beloved son. In fact, the Curé sometimes felt that his assistant was spoiling him! But he remembered his mentor, Father Balley. It had been so important to him as a young priest to be able to work with and learn from an older, wiser priest.

One day, Father Toccanier asked him, "If God gave you the choice to go to heaven or to stay on earth and continue to serve his people, what would you choose?"

"Oh, Father, that's not something I even have to think about," answered the older man. "I would stay here to do God's work!"

As the years passed, Father Vianney continued to grow weaker. It became more and more difficult to understand what he was saying when he preached. Sometimes he would fall asleep in the afternoon while hearing confessions.

Even so, he refused to give up his demanding schedule. The pilgrims would ask him for one favor after another. Some would go so far as to cut pieces from his worn-out cassock or pull the white hairs from his head. This lack of consideration angered his friends.

"Monsieur le Curé, you should just send these people away. Even the angels would not put up with such disrespect!"

The Curé never lost his simplicity or his sense of humor.

"Well my goodness," the humble priest replied, "I've been in Ars for thirty-six years. I've never acted out of anger, and I think I'm too old to start now!"

❖ ❖ ❖

On the feast of Corpus Christi in 1859, Father Vianney took part in the celebration for the last time. Every year on this special day honoring the Body and Blood of Jesus in the Blessed Sacrament, the Curé of Ars led a magnificent procession. Dressed in splendid vestments, he held the silver monstrance high and walked solemnly through the village. A huge crowd followed him amid the ringing of bells, and a chorus of voices sang their praise to God.

This year, though, Father Vianney was very weak. He couldn't carry the monstrance all the way.

"You must be very tired, Monsieur le Curé," Father Toccanier said to him afterward, handing him a glass of water.

"How could I be? It was Jesus who was carrying me."

July was a very hot month that year. Father Vianney had a sense that the end of his life was near.

On Friday, July 29, he was in the tiny confessional as usual. The heat was so intense that he could hardly breathe. He had to go out in the yard to get some fresh air.

The next morning, he was not able to get up as early as usual to be available for the sacrament of Reconciliation. He summoned Catherine and asked her to call for his confessor. After his confession, he awaited death peacefully.

His assistant, Father Toccanier, cried at his bedside. "Monsieur le Curé, surely Saint Philomena, who cured you sixteen years ago, will cure you again."

"No, God is calling me home. Saint Philomena cannot do anything this time."

On August 2, the confessor decided it was time to give Father Vianney the sacrament of Anointing of the Sick. As Father Toccanier entered the room with the Blessed Sacrament, the dying priest began to cry.

"Why are you crying?"

"Because it's sad to think this is the last time I will receive Holy Communion!"

On August 4, 1859, at two o'clock in the morning, Father John Vianney, the Curé of Ars, returned home to the God he loved so much. He was seventy-three years old, and he had been a parish priest in Ars for forty-one years.

The bells began to ring, and news of his death spread far and wide. The crowds started pouring in. This time, they came to pay their last respects to their beloved priest.

Father Vianney's example made a lasting impression on the people of Ars. Father Convert, who became the pastor of Ars thirty years after Father Vianney's death, wrote that the people who had lived in Ars at the time of the Curé lived their faith with great love. "You could have picked them out of a crowd," he said.

Father John Vianney was laid to rest in the magnificent church that had been built in Ars after his death. And on May 31, 1925, Pope Pius XI proclaimed him a saint. Four years later, on April 23, 1929, the Church declared Saint John Vianney the patron saint of all the parish priests in the world. His feast day is celebrated on August 4.

PRAYER

Saint John Vianney, you have shown us how to live our baptismal call to holiness through your life of selfless service.

You loved Jesus in the Eucharist and trusted in the help of our mother, Mary, and the saints. You worked every day to help people grow closer to God, especially through the sacraments of the Eucharist and Reconciliation.

Pray for me so that I, too, can spend my life bringing the Good News of Jesus to everyone I meet. Help me to discover and understand the vocation God is calling me to. May all priests and seminarians realize what a special calling they have received. Help them to become like Jesus.

Let your prayer be mine: "If you really love God, you will want him to be loved by the whole world."

GLOSSARY

1. **Alb**—a long white robe worn by priests and deacons during the eucharistic celebration and other liturgical functions.

2. **Benediction**—the ceremony in which a priest or deacon blesses the people with the consecrated Host enclosed in a special vessel (container) called a monstrance. The monstrance has a round window through which people can see the Sacred Host.

3. **Cassock**—a full-length black robe that may be worn by diocesan parish priests.

4. **Catacombs**—underground tunnels dug by the faithful during early Christian times in Italy. Here they buried their deceased relatives and friends.

5. **Confessor**—a priest to whom one confesses one's sins in the sacrament of Reconciliation.

6. **Confessional**—the enclosed space used for the sacrament of Reconciliation. Traditionally a screen separated the priest from the person making their confession.

7. **Conversion**—a change of heart, usually describing a person's repentance from sin.

8. **Curé**—a French term for a pastor of a parish. In this book, Saint John Vianney is referred to as Father Vianney, the Curé of Ars, or simply the Curé.

9. **Epiphany**—the feast on which we celebrate the three Wise Men presenting their gifts of gold, frankincense, and myrrh to Baby Jesus.

10. **Madame**—Mrs. in French.

11. **Mademoiselle**—Miss in French.

12. **Miracle**—a wonderful happening that goes beyond the powers of nature and is produced by God to teach us some truth or to testify to the holiness of a person.

13. **Monsieur**—Mr. in French.

14. **Ordination**—a ceremony in which a man receives the sacrament of Holy Orders. A man may be ordained a deacon, priest, or bishop.

15. **Penance**—a prayer or an action that a person says or does to express to God his or her sorrow for sin.

16. Pilgrim—a person who travels to a holy place to pray and to feel closer to God. The journey is called a pilgrimage.

17. Procession—a religious event in which people walk together from one place to another in order to publicly honor God, the Blessed Virgin, or the saints.

18. Rectory—a house where the priests of a parish live.

19. Religious Brothers or Sisters—men and women who dedicate their lives to God. They make three special promises called vows. These vows are chastity (giving up marriage), poverty (giving up personal ownership of material things), and obedience (promising to obey God's will as it comes to them through their superiors).

20. Revolution—a great social, cultural, and political upheaval begun in order to bring about a change.

21. Seminary—a school whose purpose is to educate and prepare men for the priesthood. A man attending a seminary is called a seminarian.

22. Vestments—the special garments worn by deacons, priests, or bishops for liturgical services such as the Mass, Benediction, etc.

23. **Vocation**—a call from God to a particular state in life, such as married life, single life, priesthood, or religious life. Everyone has a vocation to be holy.

Who are the Daughters of St. Paul?

We are Catholic sisters. Our mission is to be like Saint Paul and tell everyone about Jesus! There are so many ways for people to communicate with each other. We want to use all of them so everyone will know how much God loves them. We do this by printing books (you're holding one!), making radio shows, singing, helping people at our bookstores, using the Internet, and in many other ways.

Visit our website at www.pauline.org

Pauline
BOOKS & MEDIA

The Daughters of St. Paul operate book and media centers at the following addresses. Visit, call or write the one nearest you today, or find us on the World Wide Web, www.pauline.org

CALIFORNIA
3908 Sepulveda Blvd, Culver City, CA 90230 — 310-397-8676
2640 Broadway Street, Redwood City, CA 94063 — 650-369-4230
5945 Balboa Avenue, San Diego, CA 92111 — 858-565-9181

FLORIDA
145 S.W. 107th Avenue, Miami, FL 33174 — 305-559-6715

HAWAII
1143 Bishop Street, Honolulu, HI 96813 — 808-521-2731
Neighbor Islands call: — 866-521-2731

ILLINOIS
172 North Michigan Avenue, Chicago, IL 60601 — 312-346-4228

LOUISIANA
4403 Veterans Memorial Blvd, Metairie, LA 70006 — 504-887-7631

MASSACHUSETTS
885 Providence Hwy, Dedham, MA 02026 — 781-326-5385

MISSOURI
9804 Watson Road, St. Louis, MO 63126 — 314-965-3512

NEW JERSEY
561 U.S. Route 1, Wick Plaza, Edison, NJ 08817 — 732-572-1200

NEW YORK
150 East 52nd Street, New York, NY 10022 — 212-754-1110

PENNSYLVANIA
9171-A Roosevelt Blvd, Philadelphia, PA 19114 — 215-676-9494

SOUTH CAROLINA
243 King Street, Charleston, SC 29401 — 843-577-0175

TENNESSEE
4811 Poplar Avenue, Memphis, TN 38117 — 901-761-2987

TEXAS
114 Main Plaza, San Antonio, TX 78205 — 210-224-8101

VIRGINIA
1025 King Street, Alexandria, VA 22314 — 703-549-3806

CANADA
3022 Dufferin Street, Toronto, ON M6B 3T5 — 416-781-9131

¡También somos su fuente para libros,
videos y música en español!